drink.

drink.

A FOUR YEAR COMPANION

Laurie Gibson and Amanda Orr

Published in the United States by MaGu Publishing
ISBN-10: 0-692-88402-5
ISBN-13: 978-0-692-88402-7

Cover Art by Brett Hyland
Cover Layout by Penoaks Publishing, http://penoaks.com

To resisters everywhere.
Fight on.
And drink.

contents

.

"We were not a hugging people. In terms of emotional comfort it was our belief that no amount of physical contact could match the healing powers of a well made cocktail."

— DAVID SEDARIS, *NAKED*

Misery loves company so quantities
for all recipes will make two drinks.

LONG (oh such a long four years) Island Iced Tea

0.5 oz gin
0.5 oz vodka
0.5 oz spiced rum
0.5 oz tequila
0.5 oz triple sec
2 oz sweet and sour mix
12 oz cola
2 wedge lemon (optional)

Add gin, vodka, spiced rum, tequila, triple sec, and sweet and sour mix to an ice-filled Collins glass and stir. Top with cola. Garnish with lemon wedge (optional).

White Russian Puppet

Overindulge if you like. Nothing to worry about with Putin as your designated driver.

1 part Kahlua
2 parts vodka
1 part heavy cream

Fill a glass with ice cubes. Add Kahula, then vodka, then cream layer.

Mai Tai Too Long

Enough said....

3 oz spiced rum
1.5 oz coconut flavored rum
1 teaspoon grenadine syrup
6 oz pineapple juice
4 oz orange juice
2 cups ice

Combine ingredients in a cocktail shaker. Shake vigorously and strain into a glass full of ice.

Make America Grape Again

But who will pick the grapes?

White wine (super-chilled)
Club soda (cold)
Lime wedge

For this wine spritzer, fill a wine glass halfway with the super-chilled wine ... the glass should frost ... that's when you know the wine is cool enough.

Splash in the club soda until the glass is three-quarters full. (Note: You can also use ginger ale or lemon lime soda.)

Then take a slice of lime and put it on the rim of the glass.

"After the first glass, you see things as you wish they were. After the second, you see things as they are not. Finally, you see things as they really are, and that is the most horrible thing in the world."

— OSCAR WILDE

Dark and Tweet Storm

Pour one of these and fire up the
Twitter. WINNING!

4 oz dark rum
10 oz ginger beer
Lime wedge

Rum and (does he do) Coke?

Got the sniffles? This will dry them
right up.

8 oz white rum
16 oz Coca-Cola®

Serve in an old-fashioned glass.

"Alcohol is the anesthesia by which we endure the operation of life."

– GEORGE BERNARD SHAW

Hack-uiri

The perfect daiquiri for toasting
the end of privacy.

3 oz light rum
2 oz limes
2 tsp powdered sugar

Shake all ingredients with ice, strain into a cocktail glass, and serve.

Sean Spicey Bloody Mary

Hit a morning 'spin' class and then toss back a Sean Spicey at brunch.

2 parts vodka
3 parts tomato juice
¼ part Worcestershire
¼ part lemon juice
¼ part horseradish sauce
1 pinch salt
1 pinch pepper
1 pinch celery salt
2 to 4 good dashes hot sauce
2 large lime wedges
2 Pimento stuffed green olives for garnish

Take a glass and run the lime wedge around the rim to dampen. Dip top of the rim into coarse salt to completely go around the rim. Add first 8 ingredients together in the glass, squeeze the lime wedge into the glass and mix all together. Add the green olives on a toothpick, for garnish and enjoy.

"Here's to alcohol, the cause of, and solution to, all life's problems."

— THE SIMPSONS

We Are So Screw(ed) Driver

We really are...

4 oz vodka
10 oz orange juice
A pinch of salt
Orange wedge or maraschino cherry (optional)

Fill a glass (traditionally a highball) with ice, pour in your vodka and orange juice, and stir. Garnish it with a slice of orange or a maraschino cherry.

Bad Hombre Margarita

Bad.

---

3 oz tequila
1 oz premium triple sec
2 oz lime juice

Wet the rim of a cocktail glass with lime juice, and dip in salt. Shake all ingredients with ice, strain into the glass, and serve.

Hot First Lady Toddy

Perfect bedtime cocktail before
you kiss goodnight over Skype

2 oz bourbon
2 tablespoons mild honey
4 teaspoons fresh lemon juice
1/2 cup boiling-hot water

Mix bourbon, honey, and lemon juice and pour into two 6-ounce mugs. Top each with hot water and stir until honey is dissolved.

Sessions Southern Comfort Sour

No one can take away your right
to sit back and enjoy this sweet
concoction.

1 oz Southern Comfort® peach liqueur
2 oz sweet and sour mix

Can be made 'straight up' or 'on the rocks'
Prepare sour glass. Add Southern Comfort
and sour mix to mixing glass. Shake well (8-
10 times) and strain into glass providing lots
of foam. Add flag or butterfly (orange and
cherry on a pick) as garnish.

"Here's to alcohol, the rose colored glasses of life."

— F. SCOTT FITZGERALD,
THE BEAUTIFUL AND DAMNED

Nepotism Fizz

A good choice after a rough day
running the company (or the
country, oh my) with your family....

4 oz gin
juice of 1/2 lemons
2 tsp powdered sugar
2 egg
carbonated water

For this royal gin fizz, shake all ingredients
(except carbonated water) with ice and
strain into a highball glass over two ice
cubes. Fill with carbonated water, stir, and
serve.

I'll Take a Manhattan

1.5 oz sweet vermouth
5 oz bourbon whiskey
2 dash Angostura® bitters
2 maraschino cherries
2 twists orange peel

Combine the vermouth, bourbon whiskey, and bitters with 2 - 3 ice cubes in a mixing glass. Stir gently, don't bruise the spirits and cloud the drink. Place the cherries in a chilled cocktail glass and strain the whiskey mixture over the cherry. Rub the cut edge of the orange peel over the rim of the glass and twist it over the drink to release the oils but don't drop it in.

VARIATION: No bitters. Substitute a twist of lime for the cherry and orange. Hold the lime twist in a lighted match over the drink and then drop it in. The heat really zips up the lime flavor.

Fuzzy Navel

Self-tanner lotion not included

2 part peach schnapps
2 part orange juice
2 part lemonade

Mix equal parts of each ingredient in a highball glass, top with ice, and serve.

Secure the Border Pina Colada

Like pina coladas and getting caught in the rain? Don't build a wall around this tasty summer cocktail.

12 oz black rum
16 oz cream of coconut
16 oz pineapple juice
2 pineapple wedge

Combine rum, cream of coconut and pineapple juice in a regular sized blender. Blend on low speed, and fill with ice. Blend on high speed until ice is grainy. Pour into a hurricane glass, garnish with a pineapple wedge, and serve.

Slovenia Sling

Toss back one of these when
you're having writer's block and
want to get the juices flowing or...
just Google what Michelle Obama
said.

1 oz grenadine syrup
2 oz gin
sweet and sour mix
club soda
1 oz cherry brandy

Pour grenadine into the bottom of a collins glass, and fill with ice. Add gin, and almost-fill with equal parts of sweet and sour and chilled soda. Top with cherry brandy, and serve unstirred, garnished with a cherry.

"Always carry a flagon of whiskey in case of snakebite and furthermore always carry a small snake."

— W.C. FIELDS

Sex on the Beach aka Grab Her By the Pussy

Enjoy the beach while you can because with the end to all the environmental regulations, it won't be there much longer.

3 oz vodka
1 oz peach schnapps
4 oz cranberry juice
4 oz orange juice

Pour vodka and peach schnapps into a highball glass over ice. Fill with equal measures of cranberry juice and orange juice, and stir.

Conwaypolitan

If you get pulled over after drinking
a few of these, just toss out some
alternative facts.

2.5 oz vodka
0.5 oz triple sec
2 oz cranberry juice
2 lemon twist

In a shaker with ice, add vodka, triple sec,
and cranberry juice.
Shake and strain into a martini glass.
Garnish with lemon twist

Bannon Sour

4 oz brandy
juice of 1/2 lemons
1 tsp powdered sugar
1 slice lemon
2 cherries

For this brandy sour, shake brandy, lemon juice, and powdered sugar with ice and strain into a whiskey sour glass. Decorate with the lemon slice, top with the cherry, and serve.

"I have taken more out of alcohol than alcohol has taken out of me."

– SIR WINSTON CHURCHILL

Mar-a-Lago Mojito

For weekends at your winter
getaway.

2.5 oz spiced rum
24 mint leaves
2 tbsp sugar
1 oz lime juice
4 oz soda

Place mint leaves in bottom of glass. Add
crushed ice, rum, sugar, and lime juice, and
muddle. Add soda water and garnish with
mint leaves.

Bigly Hurricane

Sad.

2 oz vodka
0.5 oz grenadine syrup
2 oz gin
2 oz light rum
1 oz rum
2 oz amaretto almond liqueur
2 oz triple sec
grapefruit juice
pineapple juice

Pour all but the juices, in order listed, into a hurricane glass three-quarters filled with ice. Fill with equal parts of grapefruit and pineapple juice, and serve.

Bowling Green Martini

Still shaken up about the terrorist
attack that never happened? This
will take the edge off.

3 oz gin
1 oz dry vermouth

Stir with ice cubes, and strain into a chilled
cocktail glass. Garnish with an olive or a
twist of lemon.

"Alcohol may be man's worst enemy, but the Bible says love your enemy."

— FRANK SINATRA

Ivanka Trump's Olde Fashioned

Fashions no longer sold at Nordstroms... More bitters, fewer retailers.

4 oz bourbon whiskey
4 dashes Angostura® bitters
2 splash water
2 tsp sugar
2 maraschino cherries
2 orange wedge

Mix sugar, water and angostura bitters in an old-fashioned glass. Drop in a cherry and an orange wedge. Muddle into a paste using a muddler or the back end of a spoon. Pour in bourbon, fill with ice cubes, and stir.

Treason with a Twist

When the FBI is onto you. SAD.
Cheer up with this refreshing lemon
twist.

3 oz citron vodka
½ oz dry vermouth

Shake the vodka and vermouth with ice in a cocktail shaker. Strain into a chilled cocktail glass. Garnish with a lemon twist and serve.

Throw it All In Punch

Manage a bunch of ingredients the
way Jared Kushner manages the
entire government.

Ice
2 liter bottle of Sprite
2 cups orange juice
2 cups pineapple juice
2 cups vodka
1 bottle prosecco
2 cups strawberries sliced
2 cups raspberries
1 cup fresh mint leaves, plus more for garnish
Sanding sugars for rim

In a large punch bowl, add ice, Sprite, orange juice, pineapple juice, vodka, Prosecco, strawberries, raspberries, and mint leaves and stir to combine. Then, in a small dish of sanding sugar, rim glasses with fresh strawberry and coat rims with sugar. Ladle punch into glasses and garnish with more mint.

Don't Drain the US Mint Julep

You promised to drain the swamp,
not the Treasury

8 fresh mint sprigs
5 oz bourbon whiskey
2 tsp powdered sugar
4 tsp water

Muddle mint leaves, powdered sugar, and water in a Collins glass. Fill the glass with shaved or crushed ice and add bourbon. Top with more ice and garnish with a mint sprig. Serve with a straw.

Harvey (Bang Your Head Against the) Wall Banger

Your policies could result in my
having a serious concussion

2 oz vodka
1 oz Galliano® herbal liqueur
4 oz orange juice
ice

Pour the Vodka, Galiano, and orange juice
into a shaker with ice and shake until well
mixed. Then strain into a glass filled with ice
and serve.

"One tequila, two tequila, three tequila, floor."

— GEORGE CARLIN

Lick Your Wounds Tequila Shot

Be careful to not pour any salt in
your wounds

tequila
lime quarters
salt

Line up the shot glasses, salt and limes,
repeat...

You Golf Every Freaking Weekend Gimlet

You are a hole in one in the
hypocrite category

2.5 oz gin
2 oz Rose's® lime juice
2 twists of lime

Pour the gin and lime juice into a mixing glass half-filled with ice cubes. Stir well. Strain into a cocktail glass and garnish with the lime wedge.

Irish Coffee

Best Served with Chocolate Cake
while Bombing Syria

3 oz Irish whiskey
2 tsp brown sugar
12 oz hot coffee
heavy cream

Combine whiskey, sugar and coffee in a
mug and stir to dissolve. Float cold cream
gently on top. Do not mix.

Moscow Mule

aka Putin's Jackass

4 oz Vodka
4 oz lime juice
16 oz ginger beer

Mix ingredients in a highball glass with ice.

"My doctor told me to watch my drinking. Now I drink in front of a mirror."

– RODNEY DANGERFIELD

It's Going to Be a Tremendous Tom Collins

I mean really tremendous, just incredible

4 oz gin
2 oz lemon juice
2 tsp superfine sugar
6 oz club soda
2 maraschino cherry
2 orange slices

In a shaker half-filled with ice cubes, combine the gin, lemon juice, and sugar. Shake well. #resist the urge to shake gently. Strain into a Collins glass almost filled with ice cubes. Add the club soda. Stir and garnish with the cherry and the orange slice.

Do you Executive Order Screaming Orgasms?

No comment.

2 oz vodka
3 oz Bailey's® Irish cream
1 oz Kahlua® coffee liqueur

Pour first vodka, then Bailey's, then Kahlua into a cocktail glass over crushed ice. Stir. Caution: use only high quality vodka. Cheap vodka can cause the Bailey's to curdle. Test your brand of vodka by mixing 1 Tsp each of vodka and Bailey's first.

You Robbed Us of a Supreme Court Justice and We're Pisco Sour About It

Best served with a toast to Merrick Garland

6 parts pisco brandy
3 parts lemon juice
3 tbsp sugar

Add all ingredients to a mixer with ice. Shake well (until ice is melted), and serve in a cocktail glass.

"I used to jog, but the ice cubes kept falling out of my glass."

– DAVID LEE ROTH

Please Don't Kamikaze Bomb Korea

Please.

2.5 oz Vodka
0.5 oz triple sec
0.5 oz lime juice

Add lime juice, triple sec and Vodka.
Shake and strain into a shot glass.

Only Total Losers Don't Like Bellinis

Rosie O'Donnell, is that true?

8 oz extra dry sparkling wine
4 oz peach puree (approximately 1 pureed peach)

Pour the peach puree into the bottom of a champagne flute. Add a dash or two of grenadine or raspberry puree on the top, if you want. Gently pour dry sparkling wine to fill the glass. #resist the urge to stir For additional sweetness, dip the rims of the champagne flutes in a bowl of fine sugar, similar to how Margarita glasses are dipped in salt.

I've Lost My Appetite Spritz

Lost my appetite but gained my
marching legs

4 oz Prosecco
2.5 oz Aperol
Splash of soda water
Orange Slices

Pour Prosecco into a balloon wine glass over ice, top with Aperol and an orange slice and serve.

Release the Dossier Dead Bastard

And release your taxes while
you're at it.

2 oz brandy
2 oz bourbon whiskey
2 oz gin
2 oz rum
1 oz lime juice
2 dash bitters
2 oz ginger ale

Pour ingredients into a tall glass over ice,
stir, and serve.

Small Hands Shirley Temple

For the little ones in the family who
are also stressed about Trump.

8-12 oz ginger ale
2 oz grenadine
2 oz lime juice
2 maraschino cherry
2 orange slice

"Beer is proof that God loves us and wants us to be happy."

— BENJAMIN FRANKLIN

Wire Tap Beer

Not a cocktail person but still need to take the edge off? Not a problem. Grab a keg from your local liquor store and tap it for your buddies. But just make sure no one's listening when you share your secrets.

"There comes a time in every woman's life when the only thing that helps is a glass of champagne."

— BETTE DAVIS

I-Vana Champagne Darling

Choose your favorite bubbly and pop the cork! Let it pour down in a golden shower of celebration. No videotaping allowed.

Adios, Mother Fucker!

Let the impeachment hearings
begin!

½ oz vodka
½ oz rum
½ oz tequila
½ oz gin
½ oz Blue Curacao liqueur
2 oz sweet and sour mix
2 oz 7-Up® soda

Pour all ingredients except the 7-Up into a chilled glass filled with ice cubes. Top with soda and stir gently.

Tired of Winning Hangover Cure

This hair of the dog is perfect for the next day. And get a dog in the White House already!

6 oz gin
½ oz lemon juice
2-3 dashes hot sauce
Slice of chili pepper

Pour gin and hot sauce into an ice-filled cocktail shaker. Shake vigorously. Strain into a chilled old fashioned glass.

Cocktail Party Discussion Guide

Many say that Trump runs his White House like a reality show competition. Do you think the show will be renewed?

Trump can roll over, walk and eat solid foods. Do these milestones indicate that he is now a toddler?

One of Trump's executive orders now allows mentally ill people to buy guns. What are your thoughts now that he is legally qualified to own a firearm?

Trump says he loved his previous life and "had a lot going on." It lends the question, what exactly did he have going on?

Does Trump understand the difference between a populist and a plutocrat? Or does he think they're the same because they start with the same letter?

Since Trump's tax audit has taken so long shouldn't his first priority be modernizing the IRS?

He golfs a lot, but do we know what his handicap is? How often does he get stuck in the sand pit... or better question when isn't he in the sand pit?

Trump reportedly spends enormous amounts of time watching TV in his bathrobe. And shouldn't he honor his position as the leader of the free world, by at least watching TV in a smoking jacket?

When Ivanka Trump talks, she speaks slowly and calmly. Is this due to Valium, Xanax or too many years of listening to her father?

If we ever get to hear Jared Kushner's voice, what cartoon character do you think he is most likely to sound like?

What 'thought bubble' would best describe Chancellor Angela Merkel's reaction as she was sitting next to 'the Donald' in the Oval Office?

A lot of people are saying (I'm not sure who but many, many people have said it) that Trump and Bill O'Reilly are twins separated at birth, who in the hell are their biological parents? And how can we best punish them?

During pillow talk with his wife, what does Mike Pence says about Trump? Try to keep it clean.

During pillow talk, what does Steve Bannon reveal to his monkey?

About the Authors

Amanda Orr is an expert in gin and tonics, but under the Trump administration, she's been drinking straight from the bottle. She lives in Washington, DC, and is also the author of *A Spoonful of Sugar*.

Laurie Gibson is an entertaining dinner guest, but under the Trump administration, she rarely gets out of the fetal position. She lives in San Francisco.

For more information contact:
MaGu Publishing
magupublishing@gmail.com

Made in the USA
Middletown, DE
10 May 2017